little book of

BERLIN style

Published in 2025 by Welbeck
An Imprint of HEADLINE PUBLISHING GROUP LIMITED

1

Cataloguing in Publication Data is available from the British Library

ISBN 9781035425242

Printed and bound in China

MIX
Paper | Supporting responsible forestry
FSC® C104740

Headline's policy is to use papers that are natural, renewable and recyclable products and made from wood grown in well-managed forests and other controlled sources. The logging and manufacturing processes are expected to conform to the environmental regulations of the country of origin.

HEADLINE PUBLISHING GROUP LIMITED
An Hachette UK Company
Carmelite House
50 Victoria Embankment
London EC4Y 0DZ

The authorized representative in the EEA is Hachette Ireland,
8 Castlecourt Centre, Dublin 15, D15 XTP3, Ireland (email: info@hbgi.ie)

www.headline.co.uk
www.hachette.co.uk

AMELIE STANESCU

little book of

BERLIN style

WELBECK

CONTENTS

INTRODUCTION

Fashion in Berlin doesn't just sit on a runway; it walks the streets, sweats in the clubs and digs through flea market racks at sunrise. This isn't a city where fashion whispers about heritage or luxury. Berlin's fashion doesn't shout, it speaks in a language all of its own: a mix of grit, creativity and defiance, a refusal to be ignored. This city's style is raw, honest – and impossible to replicate because it's lived, not curated. It's a mix of history, rebellion and a little bit of chaos. You don't come to Berlin to play dress-up. You come here to figure out who you are, and maybe how you want the world to see you.

What sets Berlin apart? It's how deeply personal fashion is here. The clothes aren't just something you put on; they're loaded with meaning. They reflect the city's grit, its history, and its refusal to conform. Whether it's a vintage military jacket from a flea market, a thrifted Margiela piece you stumbled on at Final Layer, or an all-black avant-garde fit that screams Darklands, every look in Berlin feels like a statement, even when it's accidental.

But here's the thing: Berlin doesn't care if you get it. This city doesn't have that shiny, welcoming vibe you get from more polished fashion capitals. Instead, Berlin invites you to dig deeper, to pay attention to what's happening under the surface. And once you do, you start to see the threads tying it all together – history, resilience, rebellion and, honestly, a good dose of *Screw it, I'll wear what I want.*

1930s Berlin nightlife in a look: satin playsuits, military vibes and traffic lights on stage – discipline meets rebellion, cabaret meets modernity.

Berlin fashion retail in its purest form: racks of black, no distractions, no trends, just the effortless, industrial cool that keeps outsiders guessing.

Let's talk history for a second. Berlin's style DNA is tangled up in its past. From the gender-blurring cabaret scene of the 1930s to the thrift culture that rose out of post-war necessity, Berlin has always been about making something out of nothing. In the 90s, after the Wall fell, this city became a melting pot of East and West, blending Soviet utilitarianism with Western consumerism and adding a heavy dose of DIY. And then there's the club scene.

None of this is to say that Berlin is trapped by its history. Rather, it uses the past as fuel to create something entirely its own. Take its love affair with second-hand shopping. In Berlin, finding a one-of-a-kind vintage piece isn't just about style – it's a way of life. Thrift culture here is deeply embedded in the city's ethos of individuality and sustainability. It's not about following trends; it's about carving out your own identity. Shops like Homefullofclothes, Sing Blackbird Vintage and Wsiura don't just sell clothes – they sell stories. There's nothing Berliners hate more than looking like everyone else, and second-hand shopping ensures you won't.

And then there are the concept stores, which take Berlin's unpolished energy and elevate it. VOO Store is a perfect example – a place where high fashion and streetwear collide, curated so effortlessly it almost feels accidental. Or Andreas Murkudis, where minimalism reigns supreme, and every piece feels like it was hand-picked to make you rethink how you see fashion. These spaces aren't just about buying clothes; they're about creating community, sparking conversations. They're an extension of Berlin's DIY ethos, but with a polished edge that makes you stop and pay attention.

What makes Berlin so fascinating is that it doesn't try to be anything it's not. It knows exactly who it is – messy, rebellious and endlessly creative. It's a city where fashion doesn't need validation from glossy magazines or influencer-approved trends. In Berlin, it's not about fitting in; it's about standing out on your own terms. The Helmut Lang archive at Endyma, the jaw-dropping pieces at Darklands, the flea markets where you find treasure if you're willing to dig – all of it reflects a city that thrives on authenticity.

But don't mistake Berlin's independence for arrogance. It's not about being "too cool" or inaccessible. It's about making space for everyone to express themselves. Whether you're rocking a thrift jacket, an archival designer piece or something you hacked together yourself, Berlin embraces the individuality that makes its fashion scene so special. It's not about exclusivity, it's about possibility.

That's why Berlin's influence is growing. The world is finally catching on to what this city has been doing all along: putting creativity and identity first. Designers like GmbH, Namilia and Haderlump have turned Berlin's rebellious streak into global movements. These brands don't just make clothes; they make statements. They're unapologetic, pushing boundaries in ways that feel so Berlin – bold, unexpected and deeply rooted in their own vision.

But Berlin's fashion scene isn't perfect, and that's part of its charm. It's messy, sometimes disorganized and always evolving. The challenge for Berlin is to stay true to itself while navigating the pressures of the global fashion industry. Can it stay raw without becoming a caricature? Can it keep its edge while embracing the recognition it deserves? These are the questions Berlin faces as it grows – and honestly, that tension is what makes it exciting.

This book isn't here to convince you that Berlin is the best fashion city in the world. It's here to show you why it's one of the most important. In a world that feels increasingly commercialized and predictable, Berlin is a reminder of what fashion can be: deeply human. It's not about selling a dream; it's about wearing your reality and making it look damn good.

So, are you ready to step inside the world of Berlin? This is not just a city; it's a challenge. A conversation. A place that dares you to be yourself. And once you're in, you'll never see fashion – or yourself – the same way again.

Messy tailoring and combat boots: this is how Berliners do street style, like they don't care, but in a way that looks very considered.

chapter 1

WAR FASHiON

FASHION – BEFORE AND AFTER THE SECOND WORLD WAR

Berlin in the 1930s wasn't just a city; it was already a mood. Vibrant, upcoming and totally avant-garde, Berlin was fashion's playground and there were no rules. The city's energy was almost electric, crackling with a sense of rebellion and creativity that felt like it could shift the world. And it did – for a while.

Berlin was on the verge of becoming the next Paris, thanks to a perfect storm of influences: the decadent cabaret scene, the raw creativity pouring out of the Bauhaus, and an avant-garde spirit that could only exist in a city on the edge. Fashion was more than just clothes; it was a statement of identity. In the Weimar Republic, people were experimenting with who they wanted to be and how they wanted to be seen. Gender boundaries blurred in the smoky haze of underground clubs, where cross-dressing and androgyny were more than accepted – they were embraced. Berlin fashion in the early '30s was pushing boundaries just as hard as the people wearing it. Designers like Max Rée and a young Hugo Boss were starting to shape the city's look, feeding its growing love for modernity with a sense of timeless elegance. Tailoring was key – Berlin's answer to Parisian glamour but with a modern twist.

Opposite: Fashion at a polo tournament in Berlin, c.1928.

Overleaf: Women sewing garments in the costume department of production company UFA, which went on to make propaganda films for the Nazis.

Notausga

Jewish designers had a huge impact on Berlin's fashion scene. They were the backbone of the city's fashion industry – not just making clothes but creating an entire ecosystem for fashion to thrive. They perfected the business of fashion, developing a system for manufacturing and trading that was revolutionary for its time: they were running production houses, employing hundreds of people and exporting garments to other countries. Thanks to their influence, Berlin was becoming a true fashion capital with the kind of organization and infrastructure that turns fashion from an art form into an industry. By the early 1930s, Jewish-owned fashion businesses were driving Berlin's economy. In fact, they were so successful that the city's fashion scene started being compared to Paris. The Berlin-core was sleek, practical and refined – a sharp contrast to the more flamboyant styles coming out of Paris, but just as impactful.

The rise of the Nazis

Today, Hugo Boss is a name that might make you think of sharp suits and massive advertisements, but in the early 1920s, he was just a tailor trying to make a name for himself. Hugo was quick to establish himself as one of the finest tailors in Berlin, and it's impossible to talk about tailoring in the '30s without giving him any credit. His approach to craftsmanship and technical precision set him apart. Boss wasn't about bold prints or loud designs; he was all about the fit, the structure, the details that make a garment a masterpiece. He wasn't the most avant-garde designer, his work wasn't as experimental as some of his contemporaries, but he was obsessed with quality. His suits were impeccable, designed to make you feel powerful, put together and in control. Hugo built his reputation on the idea that a perfectly tailored garment wasn't just a luxury; it was a necessity.

The kind of elegance that would soon become a memory: an image by Jewish fashion photographer Yva, who was deported and murdered by the Nazis.

Berlin's shop windows became a platform for Nazi propaganda, proving that what you wear, where you shop, and who you support had now become extremely political.

At a time when German society seemed likely to implode, his work offered a sense of order, stability and refinement. His dedication to the technical aspects of tailoring – construction, fabric choice and fit – played a huge role in setting the standard for craftsmanship.

In 1931, two years before Hitler seized power, Boss joined the Nazi Party. By the following year, his factories were producing the brown shirts worn by the *Sturmabteilung* (SA), the black uniforms of the SS and the uniforms of the Hitler Youth. By 1938 he was producing uniforms for the Wehrmacht and the Waffen-SS. The rise of the Nazis changed everything – literally overnight. The fashion scene became politicized. Or rather, weaponized, reshaped to fit the Nazi ideal. The work of Boss during this time wasn't just about aesthetics – it was about creating a uniform that embodied the regime's ideals of power, discipline and control.

Boss's craftsmanship – the sharp cuts, the structured fits – became the visual language of the Nazi Party, which is why his name is controversial to this day. Yet, it's impossible to deny that Hugo Boss elevated tailoring in Berlin. His understanding of fabric, fit and craftsmanship set new standards for the industry. He took the art of tailoring and turned it into a science, something that requires discipline, precision and an obsessive eye for detail. It's a bitter irony that a man who contributed so much to Berlin's fashion legacy also played a role in one of its darkest chapters.

As the Nazis tightened their grip on the city, many of the Jewish designers who had been instrumental in building Berlin's fashion industry fled. This exodus left a massive hole in the city's creative and economic landscape. Some of these designers managed to continue their work in exile, but many were lost to history. The vibrant, diverse and experimental fashion scene that they had helped to create and which had defined Berlin in the 1920s and early '30s was gone. By the time the war started, Berlin's fashion industry was a shell of its former self, co-opted by the regime and stripped of its most brilliant talents. The fashion scene that had once been a beacon of creativity and freedom became a tool of oppression.

The legacy of 1930s Berlin fashion is complicated, a story of brilliance, resilience – and tragedy. And in that way, it's the perfect reflection of Berlin itself.

The aftermath of the Second War War

Berlin in the late 1940s wasn't glamorous; it was rubble, ration cards and broken dreams. But fashion, like the city itself, refused to die. The end of the war wasn't just about rebuilding; it was about reinventing an entire way of life. The fashion scene rose from the ashes, scrappy and unpolished, ready to redefine itself. Berlin picked up the pieces and turned them into a new style narrative, one that would set the tone for the future.

At this point, the city was divided, split into sectors controlled by the Americans, British, French and Soviets. Each sector brought its own style influences, and Berlin soaked it all up like a sponge.

The American sector was all about denim and casual wear – bringing a taste of that optimistic, consumer-driven spirit. The French, ever the epitome of chic, tried to bring a bit of Parisian glamour, even if it was muted by the city's austerity. Then there were the Brits, introducing their own sharp tailoring, trench coats and the first hints of the Mod movement. And the Soviets? They pushed uniformity and utilitarian fashion. Berliners, though, couldn't resist the allure of Western styles: wearing an American leather jacket or a British trench coat was like saying, *I want more than this rubble, I want a future.*

The war had left Berlin stripped of resources. Fabrics were scarce, and as for new clothes? Forget it. Enter the black market and the rise of what would become Berlin's iconic thrift culture. If you couldn't buy it, you made it. And if you couldn't make it, you traded for it. Berliners became pros at repurposing whatever they could get their hands on.

Surrounded by a city in ruins, a soldier in uniform walks alongside his partner in a sharp blazer and chequered skirt, a quiet act of resilience in a city learning to dress for survival.

BSR
REIN

Military uniforms got a second life as everyday wear. Wool coats were cut down into jackets, parachute silk became blouses, and leftover scraps were stitched into patchwork dresses. This wasn't just practical, it was subversive. Every piece of repurposed fabric was a silent act of defiance, a way of saying, *We're still here, and we'll look good.* Flea markets started popping up in the late 1940s, and they weren't just places to find a deal – they were community hubs, where stories, ideas and styles were traded alongside clothes. This love for vintage and second-hand wasn't just a phase; it became part of Berlin's DNA.

Creating in the shadows

While everyone was absorbing the Allied influences, a quieter revolution was happening underground. Designers who had fled Berlin during the war started trickling back, bringing with them ideas from Paris, London and New York. But starting over wasn't easy, so they went underground, literally. Hidden ateliers cropped up in basements and back rooms, where designers crafted bespoke pieces out of whatever materials they could find. One standout was Uli Richter, a quiet force in the city's couture scene and the quiet powerhouse of Berlin's post-war fashion scene. Known for his meticulous tailoring and a sharp eye for detail, Richter brought a sense of pre-war elegance back to a city that was still dusting itself off. His designs were a blend of old-world craftsmanship and new-world resourcefulness, repurposing fabrics to create silhouettes that felt both timeless and modern. He set up his

Elegance meets post-war Berlin grit: the cinched wool coat, gloves and perfectly coiffed hair might say luxury in a city learning to make fashion out of scraps.

atelier in the shadows, working away from the limelight, but his influence on Berlin's style was undeniable. He bridged the gap between the city's glamorous past and its gritty present, laying the groundwork for the experimental fashion culture that would define Berlin for decades. Richter wasn't just designing clothes: he was shaping an attitude, a quiet confidence that said, *We may be rebuilding, but we haven't lost our edge.* His designs were a blend of pre-war elegance and post-war resourcefulness: a perfect snapshot of the old Berlin meeting the new.

Women take the lead

The war flipped gender roles on their head, and fashion followed suit. With so many men lost to the conflict, women stepped into roles they'd never held before: running businesses, working in factories, leading households. Their clothes had to keep up.

Gone were the delicate dresses of the 1930s. The new look was all about practicality: high-waisted trousers, fitted blazers, sturdy shoes. This was less about looking pretty and more about getting things done. But it wasn't just about necessity; it was about empowerment. Women in Berlin weren't dressing for anyone else – they were dressing for themselves, for their work, and for the new reality they were building brick by brick. Berlin women were saying, *We don't have time for frills. We have a city to rebuild.* This shift laid the groundwork for the gender-fluid fashion for which Berlin would later become renowned.

Dressed to rebuild: sturdy coats and headscarves became the uniform of resilience in a city where survival was the priority.

Prussian-born Sonja de Lennart might not be a familiar name, but her influence was undeniable. She created Capri pants, which brought a new level of practicality to women's wardrobes, and Berlin was quick to embrace it. This was the first time that trousers were cut specifically for women, and the sleek, fitted silhouette of the Capri pants resonated with the city's minimalist, no-nonsense vibe. They were stylish yet functional – perfect for the resourceful Berlin woman who needed clothes that could transition from day to night without losing their edge. De Lennart's designs fit right into the growing trend of mixing utility with a touch of flair, paving the way for Berlin's later love of streetwear and functional fashion.

A city on the verge

By the late 1950s, Berlin was at a tipping point. The city had been rebuilt, at least on the surface, but it was still simmering with tension, caught between the pull of the East and the West. Fashion was the perfect reflection of this push and pull.

West Berlin was leaning into Western consumerism, with a love for the latest trends from the United States and Europe. Meanwhile, East Berlin embraced a more utilitarian look, influenced by the Soviet ideals of practicality and sameness. But in the underground, something else was brewing – a style that refused to fit into either box. It was raw, unpolished and uniquely Berlin.

The introduction of Capri pants in 1950s Berlin, where practicality met style, and women embraced a new kind of power dressing that was minimal and functional (but somehow modern).

chapter 2

THE BERLIN WALL

SEPARATION AND UNIFICATION

Berlin has always been a city of dualities, a place where opposites don't just coexist – they collide, mix and somehow create something entirely new. In fashion, Berlin has mastered the art of contradiction, especially when you think about how divided this city once was. In the years after the Second World War, Berlin became two worlds in one city: West Berlin, the flashy capitalist beacon of Western consumerism, and East Berlin, where socialist ideals shaped a more subdued, utilitarian way of dressing. And yet, even after a literal wall was built between them in 1961, the fashion influences didn't stay confined. Berlin's divided past created a fashion scene that today is rich with cross-cultural exchange, rebellion and innovation. So, let's dig into how East and West Berlin shaped fashion, both then and now.

Opposite: Punk became a statement in Berlin: leather jackets, ripped jeans and a DIY attitude defined a generation that refused to conform, proving that rebellion was stitched into the city's DNA.

Overleaf: Wolfgang Müller and friends at a party in West Berlin, 1984.

West vs East

Post-war West Berlin was heavily influenced by the West, especially the US, the land of freedom and rock 'n' roll. I mean, who didn't want to channel that rebellious energy coming out of American pop culture? Think about it: jeans, leather jackets and that devil-may-care attitude that came with rock 'n' roll. West Berliners were all about embracing this new wave of freedom, and you could see it in their clothes. As fashions changed over the years – influenced by mods, say, or hippies – clothes were a way to shout, *We're free, and we'll wear whatever the hell we want.* Brands like Levi's became status symbols, while second-hand shops popped up all over the place, giving the youth access to Western styles. Vivienne Westwood's punk ethos also found its way here, fuelling the city's rebellious spirit. West Berlin was all about consumerism and choice – something that would eventually clash with the grittier, more resourceful East Berlin.

Fashion in the East was about function, not flair. Socialist ideals didn't exactly leave room for extravagant self-expression, so East Berliners had to get creative. While the West was all about excess, the East embraced practicality and innovation through necessity. DIY fashion was huge – people repurposed and recycled materials because access to new clothes was seriously limited. If you wanted something fresh, you had to make it yourself. This led to a fashion scene that, while more restrained, was quietly subversive. People found ways to make fashion statements within the boundaries of the state's restrictions. Russian and Polish styles influenced the look, but it was always grounded in that Eastern Bloc sense of minimalism and utility.

East Berlin's take on power dressing: boxy silhouettes, oversized blazers and DIY tailoring that turned necessity into a quiet kind of rebellion, proving that style thrives even under restriction.

The difference between the East and the West? The West could choose excess, while the East mastered making less look like more. There was a clear tension between these two fashion worlds. Over in West Berlin, luxury and consumerism were on full display. Stores like KaDeWe (Kaufhaus des Westens) became symbols of capitalist excess, where Berliners could buy the latest global fashion trends. It was glitzy, it was exclusive and it represented everything East Berliners couldn't have. In the East, fashion was a far more rebellious affair – at least, for the younger generation. Even with the state's restrictions, young people in East Berlin were pushing boundaries, finding ways to express themselves through underground movements, secret fashion shows and illegal clubs. This era of DIY, subversive fashion laid the groundwork for the underground, club-driven aesthetic for which Berlin would later become famous. But here's the twist: despite the Wall, there was still a curiosity, a quiet exchange happening between the two sides. Fashion, like culture, doesn't obey borders, and as time went on, the influences started seeping through.

Levi's, T-shirts featuring Western bands, leather jackets – these were all smuggled into East Berlin and became the ultimate symbols of rebellion and aspiration. If you had a piece of Western fashion in the East, this was more than a style statement – it was a political one. The black market for Western fashion was alive and well, and for those who could get their hands on it, these clothes represented freedom, individuality and access to a world beyond the Wall. This exchange wasn't all one-sided, either. As tensions between East and West grew, so did curiosity. Westerners began to look East, fascinated by the utilitarian, minimalist aesthetic that had evolved out of necessity. And East Berliners, despite the restrictions, found ways to create their own versions of Western trends.

Above: West Berlin's fashion became a symbol of everything that lay just out of reach for the East.

Overleaf: East Berlin punk versus old-school pragmatism DIY street fashion colliding with conservative tailoring.

FLORENA

In this divided city, Klaus Jürgen Schumann was one of the few designers who saw the Berlin Wall not as a barrier but as a challenge. Operating out of West Berlin, he had a knack for blending sleek Western styles with the practical aesthetic that defined the East. Schumann's designs were a quiet rebellion against the rigid fashion norms of both sides. His collections featured sharp lines, a mix of structured blazers with casual, oversized knits and a hint of androgyny that foreshadowed Berlin's future obsession with gender-fluid fashion, and echoed its experimental past. By collaborating with East Berlin designers and drawing inspiration from Soviet fashion, Schumann created a unique visual language that spoke to the duality of the divided city. He was proof that, no matter how high you build a wall, you can't stop cultural exchange.

The fall of the Wall

And then came the year of 1989. The Wall fell, and suddenly, East and West weren't just meeting, they were clashing. The fashion worlds of East and West collided in the best way possible, creating a hybrid scene that still defines Berlin today. The fashion scene became a melting pot of global influences. Military jackets, repurposed workwear, bold prints – everything was up for grabs. The city's fashionistas started mixing Western consumerism with the DIY culture of the East. Vintage stores were thriving, and international designers started paying attention. Berlin wasn't just a city picking up the pieces after reunification – it was becoming a style capital in its own right. Designers from the East began gaining recognition while Western brands started referencing the raw, unpolished style of the East in their collections. The result? Berlin's ability to seamlessly blend influences from both sides of the Wall into something entirely its own.

The Berlin Wall comes down and so do the barriers in fashion: East meets West in a chaotic, beautiful clash of styles, proving that in Berlin, culture and love will always outlive division.

Nor is this ethos a thing of the past – it's alive and well today, constantly evolving with new influences, new designers and new ways of thinking about fashion. Whether you're rocking a second-hand military jacket or a designer dress, one thing is for sure: in Berlin, fashion is more than just what you wear – it's a reflection of who you are, where you've been and where you're going. Berlin isn't just a city: it's a style revolution that's still unfolding.

chapter 3

MAKING BERLIN

BOWIE, IGGY POP AND REINVENTION

Berlin in the late 1970s was rough around the edges, a city still grappling with its past while caught in the tension of the Cold War. But if there's one thing Berlin knows how to do, it's turn chaos into creativity. Enter David Bowie and Iggy Pop, two rock legends who found a new home in this gritty landscape. Their arrival wasn't just a blip on Berlin's cultural radar, it was a seismic shift that would redefine the city's fashion identity. They didn't just bring their music; they brought a style and attitude that synced perfectly with Berlin's underground spirit at that time.

When Bowie landed in Berlin in 1976, he was looking for a fresh start, a break from the excess and glitz of his life in the US. In the shadowy streets of Schöneberg, he found exactly what he needed. Berlin was raw, unfiltered and unpretentious, and Bowie didn't just adapt to the city's vibe; he embodied it, ditching his Ziggy Stardust costumes for something more pared down: oversized blazers, slim trousers, crisp white shirts. It was minimal, sleek and a little mysterious – just like the city itself.

A young Bowie came to Berlin and redefined underground fashion with a mix of androgynous cool and raw, unfiltered rebellion.

Bowie's style shift wasn't just a personal reinvention; it was a nod to Berlin's no-nonsense approach to fashion. He leaned into androgynous looks and understated cool, swapping sequins for sharp tailoring and clean lines. And Berlin noticed. Local designers started picking up on his new look, incorporating elements like oversized blazers and monochrome palettes into their collections. Bowie's influence elevated the underground style scene, making it aspirational. His tailored yet gender-fluid outfits paved the way for what we now call Berlin-core: a mix of minimalist, androgynous fashion that became the city's signature look.

While Bowie brought the cool, Iggy Pop brought the chaos. He showed up in Berlin like a whirlwind, all ripped jeans, leather jackets and zero care for convention. Iggy wasn't about looking polished; he was about looking real. His style was punk before punk had fully solidified as a movement, and Berlin was the perfect place for it. He found his scene in Kreuzberg's dive bars and punk clubs like SO36, where the dress code was as raw as the music.

Iggy's aesthetic was a perfect fit for a city that was tired of polished, consumer-driven fashion. His look was loud and messy – torn jeans, combat boots, shirtless performances. It was pure rebellion, and Berlin's youth ate it up. Iggy's scrappy DIY look felt authentic.

Young Berliners started mimicking his style, ripping their jeans, scuffing their leather jackets and adopting that attitude of *I don't give a damn*. It wasn't just about the clothes; it was about rejecting the polished, picture-perfect ideal coming out of the West. Iggy became a fashion icon for Berlin's misfits, the kids who wanted to wear their rebellion on their sleeves, literally.

Above: Before punk had a rulebook, Iggy was already breaking all the rules, making Berlin the perfect stage fcr his raw, DIY style.

Overleaf: Bowie in Hansa music studio wearing leather. His attitude and style quickly became iconic in Berlin.

magnetophon

TELEFUNKEN

SO36
ABENDKASSE
13 EUR

Bowie and Iggy were like Berlin's yin and yang: Bowie with his sleek sophistication, Iggy with his raw, chaotic energy. The synergy between them was palpable, and their influence soon rippled through Berlin's fashion scene. They were often spotted together at Hansa Studios, recording Bowie's album *Heroes* and mixing Iggy's *The Idiot* and leaving a trail of stylish moments behind them.

What made their partnership so electric was how their styles fed off each other. Bowie's tailored, androgynous looks collided with Iggy's punk aesthetic, creating a unique fashion mashup that felt distinctly Berlin. Local designers started blending these elements – sharp cuts paired with distressed fabrics, tailored pieces mixed with DIY punk details. It was a new kind of cool that could only have come from the collision of these two rock icons.

Bowie and Iggy weren't just setting trends; they were creating a whole new visual language for Berlin's underground. A mix of elegance and chaos, and a reflection of a city that was always teetering on the edge but never quite falling apart.

The Club Scene: where fashion found its beat

Berlin's nightlife in the late '70s was about losing yourself in the music, the crowd and the fashion experiments that came alive after dark. Clubs like Dschungel and SO36 weren't just places to dance; they were fashion incubators where the city's underground style was on full display. And Bowie and Iggy were right at the heart of it.

Nightlife became a breeding ground for fashion, where ripped jeans, safety pins and oversized knits were just as much a part of the scene as the sound of the underground.

In these clubs, fashion wasn't just an outfit – it was a statement. The city's love for black clothing, military surplus and leather was part practicality, part rebellion. It was a uniform of defiance, a way of saying, *We're not here to conform.* Bowie's tailored blazers mingled with Iggy's ripped jeans, creating a visual contrast that spoke to the city's love of blending opposites.

The club scene also became a testing ground for new looks. Fetish fashion started creeping into the mainstream here, influenced by the city's emerging queer scene. Leather harnesses, PVC and bondage-inspired accessories began to appear alongside the punk and androgynous styles that Bowie and Iggy popularized. It was Berlin doing what it does best: mixing things up, pushing boundaries and creating something entirely its own.

The time Bowie and Iggy spent in Berlin was short but transformative, changing the city's fashion DNA. Bowie's androgynous elegance laid the groundwork for Berlin's gender-fluid fashion movement, while Iggy's punk rawness set the stage for the DIY, unpolished aesthetic that still defines the city's street style today. But it's not just about the clothes, it's about the attitude. Bowie and Iggy brought a sense of freedom, a permission to experiment, and a fearlessness that Berlin has never let go. They showed the city that style isn't about playing by the rules; it's about breaking them, mixing the polished with the rough, and wearing whatever makes you feel like you.

That's the legacy of Bowie and Iggy in Berlin. Here, fashion isn't about fitting in – it's about standing out, and that's exactly what Bowie and Iggy taught us. In a city that's always on the edge of something new, their influence is still felt, a reminder that the coolest look you can wear is one that doesn't care what anyone else thinks.

Stickers, slogans and raw, rebellious graphics on a club's bathroom wall, reflecting Berlin's club scene as a space where fashion, music and counterculture all clashed and thrived.

chapter 4

THE 1990S

Above: Fashion exuding the wild, uninhibited energy of the underground nightlife.

Overleaf: As men's style became more and more androgynous, fashion became a way of self-expression, including sexual expression.

CHAOS AND CREATIVITY COLLIDE

The 1990s in Berlin were a decade of transition and tension, when the scars of division clashed with the boundless optimism of reunification. The city was raw, messy and brimming with potential. Berlin was not concerned with conforming to fashion capitals like Paris or Milan. Instead, it thrived on its imperfections, using them as fuel to create a new visual language that would go on to influence global trends. This period wasn't about following fashion norms, it was about creating new ones to fit a city thriving on chaos. The reunification of East and West catalyzed a unique cultural exchange that reshaped Berlin's identity and its place in the fashion world.

The fall of the Berlin Wall in 1989 set the stage for a decade defined by hybridity. The gritty, utilitarian aesthetic of East Berlin merged with the experimental and consumer-driven influences of the West. Streetwear emerged not as a trend but as a necessity. Military surplus stores became hotspots, offering affordable and durable clothing that Berliners repurposed into their wardrobes. East Berlin's practicality met West Berlin's love for customization, resulting in patched-together bomber jackets, oversized trench coats and combat boots that could withstand hours in the city's clubs. DIY couture became the unofficial uniform of the creative class. Fabric scraps, thrift store finds and even household items were transformed into wearable art. Berliners weren't just consumers; they were makers, deconstructing and reconstructing garments to reflect their individuality. This

hands-on approach to fashion echoed the city's broader ethos: if the system isn't working for you, break it apart and make it your own.

The 1990s were the golden age of Berlin's underground club scene. After the Wall fell, abandoned spaces in East Berlin became the epicentres of nightlife. Clubs like Tresor and E-Werk weren't just venues for music; they were laboratories for self-expression. Inside these industrial spaces, fashion was stripped down to its core, a means of survival and identity. Black became the dominant colour palette, not because it was trendy but because it was practical. In the dimly lit, sweat soaked basements, black clothing absorbed the grime and blended seamlessly with the shadows. Leather, mesh and PVC were popular choices, inspired by fetish wear but adapted for the dance floor. Harnesses and straps weren't just accessories; they were declarations of individuality. Berliners embraced a "techno uniform" that balanced utility and rebellion. Platform boots, cargo pants and oversized hoodies became staples, designed to endure long nights of dancing while rejecting the polished aesthetics of mainstream fashion. The unspoken rule of Berlin club fashion was simple: wear what makes you feel invincible, and leave pretension at the door.

Berlin in the 1990s was a breeding ground for subcultures, each with its own distinct style. Punk, which had taken root in West Berlin during the 1980s, found new energy in the post-Wall era. Mohawks, studded leather jackets and DIY patches became symbols of defiance in a city still grappling with its identity. The rave culture that blossomed alongside the techno scene brought its own sartorial statements. Fluorescent colours, reflective materials and chunky sneakers contrasted sharply with the darker aesthetics of the techno crowd. These styles often collided at the city's many open-air raves, where boundaries between subcultures blurred in the shared pursuit of freedom and self-expression. Queer fashion also thrived during this period, with drag and androgyny taking centre stage in the city's queer nightlife scene. Clubs like SchwuZ and the legendary Ostgut became safe spaces for experimentation, where traditional notions of gender and beauty were challenged and redefined. Sequins, feathers and avant-garde makeup were as common as leather and latex, showcasing the city's commitment to celebrating individuality.

Above: Loose-fitting clothing, dark silhouettes and oversized rave essentials blending into the haze of Berlin's '90s techno culture.

Overleaf: Harald Blüchel (aka Cosmic Baby) DJing at iconic techno club Tresor, 1993.

The impact of reunification

Reunification didn't just reunite families, it collided two distinct cultural aesthetics. West Berlin brought its affinity for Western consumerism, with brands like Levi's and Adidas gaining traction among the youth. East Berlin contributed a minimalist, resourceful approach to fashion, born out of necessity during years of restricted access. This exchange wasn't always harmonious. For some, Western brands represented a loss of individuality; for others, they were symbols of freedom and progress. However, the tension between these perspectives ultimately enriched Berlin's fashion identity. Designers began to experiment, blending Western logos with Eastern-inspired silhouettes, and creating a dialogue between excess and restraint. Vintage stores also became critical players in this new fashion landscape. These stores weren't just places to shop; they were hubs for cultural exchange, where Berliners pieced together looks that celebrated their city's diversity.

By the end of the decade, Berlin's fashion scene had caught the attention of international designers and media. The city's unpolished, rebellious aesthetic stood in stark contrast to the opulence of Paris or the commercialism of New York. Designers like Raf Simons and Alexander McQueen began to reference Berlin's underground culture in their collections, borrowing elements like distressed fabrics, oversized silhouettes and utilitarian details. Berlin's influence extended beyond the runway. The rise of streetwear in the late 1990s and early 2000s owes much to the DIY ethos and urban grit of Berlin fashion. Brands like Supreme and Off-White, which emphasize individuality and subversion, can trace their roots back to the kind of anti-fashion statements that defined Berlin in the 1990s.

This was the decade that laid the foundation for Berlin's reputation as a global fashion hub. The decade's emphasis on individuality, resourcefulness and rebellion continues to shape the city's fashion identity. Berlin remains a place where rules are meant to be broken, where the past informs the present without dictating it, and where fashion is as much about attitude as it is about aesthetics. This era also cemented Berlin's status as a city where anyone could belong. Whether you were a punk in a studded jacket, a club kid in a harness or a minimalist in all black, Berlin in the 1990s was a place where you could find your tribe – and your style.

A Raf Simons piece from 1998, embodying Berlin's anti-fashion attitude where imperfection, decay and repurposing are not flaws but stylistic choices.

Above and opposite: One of Alexander McQueen's most iconic shows, A/W 1996, showcases the rawness that was resonating with the Berlin underground style at the time. From fishnets to raw cuts, this could be a scene from any club in Berlin at that time.

Above: Alexander McQueen S/S 1996, where razor-sharp tailoring met brutal deconstruction, mirroring '90s Berlin

Opposite: Hannelore Knuts in Ruffo Research S/S 1999. Sharp, industrial and stripped of excess, the look embodies Berlin in the late '90s.

chapter 5

CLUBBING

Let's be real: Berlin's clubbing scene isn't just about music – it's a lifestyle. It's about stepping into a world where everything is raw, authentic and a little bit chaotic. That chaos? It's magic, especially when it comes to fashion. From the dark and industrial spaces of Berghain to the neon-soaked raves of the '90s, Berlin's nightlife has always been a space for self-expression, a space for people to dress without judgement, and ultimately, to push fashion boundaries. And this energy has not only shaped how Berliners dress – it's influenced global fashion in ways that are undeniable. To understand how Berlin's clubbing scene has shaped fashion, we need to dive into the gritty, haunting world of *Zoo Station: The Story of Christiane F.*

The autobiography of a teenage girl trapped in a world of drugs and addiction around Berlin's Bahnhof Zoo station is more than just a shocking tale – it's a cultural touchstone. Developed into a film that was released in 1981, it has since become a cult classic, and for designers like Raf Simons and countless others, it became a symbol of a certain kind of Berlin aesthetic: one that's dark, raw and, somehow, still alluring. When *Christiane F.* hit the scene, it wasn't just a book – it was a vibe. Berlin in the '70s and '80s was a city caught between East and West, between political tension and creative freedom. *Zoo Station* captured this perfectly: the gritty underbelly of a divided city, where lost youth wandered

Opposite: A raver lost in the moment under neon lights embodies the city's club culture.

Overleaf: Natja Brunckhorst portraying Christiane F. in the 1981 film *Christiane F. – Wir Kinder vom Bahnhof Zoo.*

WASTED
GERMAN
YOUTH

through abandoned buildings, experimenting with drugs and searching for a sense of belonging. And fashion? It was a reflection of that existential crisis. The kids in *Christiane F.* didn't care about labels or trends – they wore whatever they could find, whether that was a beat-up leather jacket, tattered jeans, or oversized sweaters that looked like they had been through hell. This wasn't about looking polished; it was about survival. The look became iconic because it was so real – a rejection of the shiny, consumer-driven fashion world. It was the ultimate anti-fashion statement.

Raf Simons saw something profound in this aesthetic. Known for drawing inspiration from youth culture, he has referenced *Christiane F.* in his work, transforming that raw, rebellious energy into high fashion. His collections often feel like they're pulled straight from Berlin's underground scene, with oversized silhouettes, dark colour palettes and a sense of melancholic defiance. It's that juxtaposition – something that looks "wrong" but which feels oh-so-right – that Berlin's clubbing scene is all about. And *Zoo Station* became the blueprint.

The Berlin clubbing scene is not about dressing to impress – it's about dressing to be free. In the '90s, when techno first exploded in Berlin, the city's underground spaces became a haven for people who wanted to escape the ordinary. The abandoned warehouses, the DIY raves, the sense that you could wear whatever you wanted as long as it made you feel something – this was the heartbeat of Berlin fashion. Berlin's club fashion is rooted in function, but with a heavy dose of rebellion. Think oversized bomber jackets, military surplus gear, platform boots that could survive hours on the dance floor, and lots of black. Always black. Minimalist, but with an edge. And not just about looking cool, but about being ready

A clubgoer in Berlin wears a bold "Wasted German Youth" T-shirt. On the underground scene, fashion isn't about perfection but about survival, defiance and belonging.

Above: Raf Simons takes his runway bow wearing a shirt emblazoned with the face of Christiane F.

Opposite: Raf Simons A/W 2018.

Above: Rick Owens embodies the city's raw, utilitarian edge with this dark, oversized tailoring – blurring the line between clubwear and high fashion, just like Berlin itself.

Overleaf: Rick Owens A/W 2018 Menswear.

for anything. In Berlin, you dress to survive the night, the rain, the flashing lights, the pounding bass, the city. And that's what makes Berlin's fashion scene so unique: it's practical, but never boring.

Let's not forget the fetish influence: clubs like Berghain and KitKatClub have blurred the lines between clubwear and fetish fashion, with leather harnesses, PVC and bondage-inspired accessories becoming part of the city's style. In the darkness of the club, there are no rules – just freedom to experiment, to be whoever you want to be, even if that means stripping down to nothing but boots and a harness. This underground, rebellious spirit caught the attention of fashion designers around the world. Berlin's clubbing scene became a reference point for anyone looking to inject a sense of raw realness into their collections. It's no coincidence that designers like Alexander McQueen and Hedi Slimane have cited Berlin's underground culture as an inspiration. The city's club scene, with its "anything goes" attitude, offered an alternative to the polished, commercial fashion world. It was messy, chaotic and authentic – and that's exactly what made it so irresistible.

Berlin has never really cared about being fashionable – and that's what made it so influential. The underground clubs, the dark techno beats, the self-made and self-organized raves – these weren't spaces designed to attract the fashion crowd. They were designed for people to escape. But fashion, as it always does, found its way in. By the mid-2000s, Berlin's club fashion had gone global. Designers like Rick Owens and Raf Simons started incorporating elements of Berlin's underground scene into their collections, turning what had once been anti-fashion into high fashion. The oversized coats, the minimalist black ensembles, the utilitarian workwear – it all echoed the styles you'd see on a Saturday night at Berghain. But it's not just about the clothes. It's about the attitude. Berlin fashion has always been about

RSC

Above and opposite: Raf Simons' deconstructed, oversized silhouettes and raw graphics channel the anarchic spirit of Berlin's club culture – where fashion isn't just about aesthetics, but about making a statement in the underground.

breaking the rules, and designers everywhere can relate to that. The clubbing scene in Berlin doesn't follow trends – it creates them. It's the birthplace of looks that challenge the status quo, that say, "I don't care what you think," while still looking effortlessly cool.

The influence of Berlin's club scene didn't stop with high fashion. It bled into streetwear, with brands like GmbH emerging from the city's underground, blending club culture with political statements. GmbH, founded by Berlin-based designers Serhat Isik and Benjamin Huseby, is the perfect example of how Berlin's club fashion has evolved into something that's not just about aesthetics, but is about identity, politics and culture. Their collections are rooted in the spirit of Berlin's clubs, where diversity, inclusion and freedom are celebrated through fashion.

If you want more proof of just how much Berlin's clubbing scene has shaped fashion, look no further than Sven Marquardt, the bouncer at Berghain, who's become one of the city's biggest fashion icons. The gatekeeper to the coolest club in town, he's also a walking embodiment of Berlin's underground style. With his tattooed face, silver beard and intense gaze, Sven is a legend in his own right. Facing him at Berghain's door isn't just about getting into a party – it's the ultimate test of whether you're bold enough to step into the wildest night of your life. Bouncer by night and fashion photographer by day, he has that distinct brutalist style that's so much intertwined with the style of the city.

Opposite: The famous/infamous bouncer Sven Marquardt of the most famous techno club in the world, Berghain.

Overleaf: Sven Marquardt has been a pivotal figure in the city's nightlife and scene since the club's inception in 2004. Beyond his role at Berghain, Marquardt is an accomplished fashion photographer.

MAYA

chapter 6

BERLiN
FASHiON
WEEK

МИР
PEACE

A REBEL WITH A CAUSE

Let's get one thing straight: Berlin Fashion Week wasn't born to compete with Paris or Milan. It was born to disrupt them. Back in 2007, when Berlin threw itself into the global fashion calendar, the fashion elite wasn't exactly holding its breath. Berlin wasn't known for runways and couture, it was known for club kids, graffiti and the kind of creative energy that could fuel a thousand revolutions.

But Berlin doesn't wait for permission. And unlike its more polished cousins, this wasn't about tradition or heritage, mainly because Berlin doesn't really have either. This was about invention, rebellion and proving that fashion can exist outside the confines of gilded line sheets. Fuelled by the city's DIY core, Berlin Fashion Week scratched and clawed its way into existence. Funding was secured when the German government and Berlin Senate saw an opportunity, alert to the potential for creative industries to bring in the cash, and Mercedes-Benz stepped in as the official sponsor. Fashion Week hit the ground running.

Opposite: Jean Gritsfeldt's show in 2022 at Berlin Fashion Week, standing against the Russian invasion of Ukraine.

Overleaf: Berlin Fashion Week transforms the city's industrial spaces into a stage for experimental style, where avant-garde designers, underground aesthetics and the raw energy of Berlin's club culture collide to redefine fashion on their own terms.

Without a century of haute couture history to lean on, it made up its own rules. The early days were chaotic in the best way. Runways popped up in abandoned warehouses, art galleries and even clubs. Shows felt more like performances, blurring the lines between fashion, art and nightlife. Designers weren't just showcasing clothes; they were creating entire worlds, inspired by Berlin's underground scenes, from techno to street art. This wasn't fashion for fashion's sake – it was fashion with a cause.

Berlin Fashion Week became a platform for voices often overlooked in traditional fashion capitals. Sustainability wasn't a buzzword here; it was baked into the DNA of many collections. Designers like Haderlump are turning discarded materials into high fashion, while Namilia is using their shows to deliver politically charged messages about sexuality and power. This is a reminder that Berlin does not just follow trends: it interrogates them, challenges them and, when necessary, burns them to the ground.

In the global fashion world, Berlin's arrival wasn't met with immediate acceptance. Critics scoffed at its lack of polish, and a vibe that was "rough around the edges". But that's the thing about Berlin: the city thrives on being underestimated. Over time, Berlin Fashion Week carved out a space for itself not by trying to replicate Parisian glamour or Milanese sophistication, but by doubling down on its own identity: bold, innovative and a little bit chaotic.

Opposite: Street style in Berlin: Amelie Stanescu.

Overleaf: Danny Reinke S/S 2025.

By the 2010s, Berlin Fashion Week had evolved into a global stage for emerging designers, a playground for avant-garde experimentation, and a rallying point for sustainability and inclusivity. It became less about competing with the old guard and more about creating its own lane. Now, Berlin Fashion Week is a force to be reckoned with, a reflection of the city: a melting pot of cultures, ideas and unfiltered creativity. It doesn't want to be Paris or Milan, and that's exactly why we can't stop watching.

Above: Models on the runway during the DZHUS show during Berlin Fashion Week S/S 25 – an example of Berlin's experimental fashion.

Opposite: Body, materiality and perception at Marina Hoermanseder A/W 24: Berlin fashion has always embraced radical self-expression, and this runway moment feels like a perfect intersection of fetish aesthetics, performance art and the city's rejection of conventional beauty norms.

From underdog to global subverter

In its early years, Berlin Fashion Week was seen as the scrappy underdog of the fashion world. But here's the thing: Berlin doesn't care about being liked, and that indifference is its secret weapon. Over time, Berlin Fashion Week evolved into something even the most sceptical fashion insiders couldn't ignore. The city became a playground for innovators and rule-breakers, where tech collides with textiles and sustainability isn't a buzzword but a way of life. International buyers and editors who once dismissed Berlin as too edgy now flock to see what's next. And it's not just about the runway shows. Berlin Fashion Week has become a platform for serious cultural dialogue. Tech integration, gender fluidity, political statements and constant innovation is what diversifies this fashion week from the rest. Today, it is perceived as the rebel of the global fashion scene, the place where the next generation of designers cut their teeth.

You won't see a front row overflowing with Hollywood A-listers or socialites at Berlin Fashion Week. Instead, it's filled with creatives, artists and thinkers – people who genuinely care about the designs coming down the runway rather than how they look sitting beside it. The energy here is raw and refreshingly authentic, focused on innovation and ideas rather than exclusivity or star power. Where other fashion weeks thrive on closed doors and carefully curated guest lists, this event runs on openness. It's a space where designers, students and even underground artists can find a platform.

Berlin street style: Amelie Stanescu walking through the city like a dystopian warrior.

D

Berlin Fashion Week is where contrasts thrive – decadence and casual grit collide, proving that individuality always wins over conformity.

What sets this fashion week apart is its accessibility, a quality that flips the script on traditional fashion capitals. Paris, Milan, London and New York – the Big Four – operate on a currency of status and privilege, where the front row is as much a battlefield as the runway itself. Here, the value lies in inclusion. The audience is a mix of people passionate about design, unafraid of bold ideas and eager to break the rules. It's not about who you are but what you bring to the conversation.

This philosophy has created a hub for creativity to flourish without traditional gatekeeping. The inclusive nature isn't just refreshing – it's strategic. By inviting a wide range of voices to speak, the event has become a hotbed for experimentation, where ideas that would be deemed too risky elsewhere are embraced. The result is a fashion week that feels alive and full of potential, carving its own path in the global fashion scene. It's not about polished perfection; it's about authenticity, pushing boundaries and redefining what a runway can represent. This space is where the future of style is being shaped, not by the faces in the crowd but by the radical visions on display.

Being accessible is what made Berlin fashion become a thing: the currency for the established Big Four is exclusivity, the currency for Berlin is inclusivity. In addition, the venues are iconic: runways set up in industrial warehouses, presentations in sprawling graffiti-covered buildings, after-parties that start at 2 a.m. and spill into the city's legendary clubs. Every inch of Berlin Fashion Week screams, *We're not here to fit in*. And then there's the fashion itself. Berlin designers don't play it safe. This is the city of gender-fluid silhouettes, anarchist couture and sustainable innovation. This is where where punk meets minimalism, streetwear meets high fashion, and the boundaries between art and clothing blur into oblivion.

Above and opposite: Drenched in black but never blending in – Berlin's street style is all about power dressing with an edgy high fashion.

Above: Namilia doesn't whisper – it screams, flipping Berlin's underground into pop culture rebellion with bold slogans and unapologetic excess.

Overleaf: Paris Hilton and Teyana Taylor walk for Namilia in 2018.

The brands leading the charge

Namilia – *punk couture* on steroids

Namilia doesn't just march to the beat of its own drum: it smashes the drum, sets it on fire and builds a runway out of the ashes. Founded by Nan Li and Emilia Pfohl, this brand is Berlin's wild child. Their designs are provocative, political and proudly over the top, flipping off tradition at every turn.

Namilia's collections are performance art, blending BDSM-inspired silhouettes, cartoonish proportions and slogans that make you stop in your tracks. They don't just dress their models, they arm them for battle, reclaiming narratives about female sexuality, power and rebellion.

In 2023, the brand made global headlines for a messy, headline-grabbing showdown with luxury giant Hermès, proving yet again that they don't just shake the table – they flip it. The controversy started when their collection Her Mess debuted. The line featured satirical designs that twisted Hermès' iconic imagery, blending bondage aesthetics with tongue-in-cheek humour aimed squarely at the luxury industry's untouchable elite. Bags resembling the infamous Birkin, but dripping in PVC, chains and slogans, sent a clear message: luxury isn't sacred, and it's definitely not above critique. Hermès, unsurprisingly, wasn't laughing. Legal teams were mobilized, cease and desist letters flew, and fashion insiders watched the drama unfold like a reality show. Namilia, true to form, doubled down. Their response? A cheeky Instagram post featuring a model handcuffed to a knock-off Birkin. Message received.

For Namilia, the scandal wasn't a setback, it was fuel and it was marketing. They didn't just survive the Hermès backlash; they thrived on it, gaining even more attention for their refusal to back down.

If the Hermès feud proved Namilia's rebellious spirit, their collaboration with Khy (Kylie Jenner's streetwear line) showed they could play the mainstream game without losing their edge. The partnership launched in late 2023, with a capsule collection that merged Khy's commercial savvy with Namilia's signature shock factor. The collab featured oversized silhouettes, graphic prints and fetish-inspired details toned down just enough for mass appeal but still dripping with Namilia's anarchic DNA. It was a power move, catapulting the brand into the global spotlight. Kylie Jenner modelling a latex bustier with a Namilia logo? That's the kind of visibility that can make or break you. Luckily it didn't break Namilia. This wasn't just about clothes but also about introducing Namilia's ethos to a whole new audience. Suddenly, the brand was everywhere: featured in *Vogue*, splashed across TikTok, and making headlines on every fashion blog worth reading. The collab marked a turning point, transforming Namilia from an underground favourite into a global icon.

What makes Namilia so compelling isn't just their clothes, it's the unapologetic attitude behind them. This is a brand that understands fashion as a weapon, a tool for rebellion and a platform for cultural commentary. They're here to challenge the establishment, piss people off, and look damn good doing it. From the Hermès scandal to their Khy collab, Namilia has proven they can take on the industry's biggest players without losing their soul. And in Berlin, a city that thrives on disruption, that makes them nothing short of iconic.

Above: The infamous Namilia collection that sent shockwaves through the fashion world featured satirical Hermès-inspired designs.

Overleaf: Age, gender and convention don't matter here – Berlin Fashion Week rewrites the rules of who gets to be iconic.

BABY
AMORE
Silentium

Haderlump – turning scraps into statements

Haderlump is Berlin distilled into a brand: scrappy, unpolished and boundary-breaking. Founded by Johann Ehrhardt, even its name – "good-for-nothing" – is a middle finger to the glossy perfection of traditional fashion. (The word was originally coined to describe the travellers who collected rag in the eighteenth and nineteenth centuries to sell to paper mills.) Haderlump doesn't just make clothes; it creates wearable art out of the scraps everyone else leaves behind, proving that trash really can become treasure.

Haderlump doesn't preach sustainability – it lives it. The brand's DNA is rooted in turning waste into wonder: decommissioned workwear, forgotten deadstock fabrics and materials that most would toss without a second thought. Think patchwork denim that looks like it survived an apocalypse but somehow came out cool; asymmetrical cuts that defy symmetry in the best way; and textures that scream, *Dare to look closer*. Each piece is raw, one of a kind, and utterly Haderlump.

The atelier isn't just a workspace; it's a shrine to the brand's ethos. Every piece is designed and crafted on-site. Walking into the space, you feel the heartbeat of the brand: a mix of rebellion, resourcefulness and undeniable craft.

In February 2024, the brand hit peak innovation with its Circularis collection. Partnering with DHL (yes, the courier giant), it transformed old uniforms into a statement collection. Red and yellow became runway ready, proving that corporate utilitarianism and high fashion can coexist. The pieces were wearable, yet at the same time they presented a manifesto on how fashion can innovate without destroying the planet.

Domiziana attends the Haderlump fashion show
as part of Berlin Fashion Week A/W 24.

Above and opposite: Haderlump took the city's rebellious DNA to new heights – literally – by staging their AERO collection at Tempelhof Airport, where aviation history met subversive fashion, proving once again that Berlin's runways aren't just for planes.

Sven Marquardt, the gatekeeper of Berlin's nightlife, brought his signature presence to Haderlump's AERO show at Tempelhof Airport.

Just months later, in July 2024, the brand delivered a showstopper at the legendary Tempelhof Airport. AERO, a collection inspired by aviation and freedom, unfolded against the backdrop of vintage aircraft. Over 700 guests witnessed the spectacle, cementing Haderlump as more than a brand: it's a cultural force.

Olivia Ballard – quiet power in a loud world

Olivia Ballard might seem like the odd one out in Berlin's cacophony of experimental fashion, but her minimalist aesthetic speaks volumes. Originally from New York, Ballard brings a quiet sophistication to the city's fashion scene. Her designs are sleek, introspective and deeply personal, offering a counterbalance to the chaos around her.

Originally from New York, Ballard brings a poetic, introspective energy to Berlin's chaotic mix.

Above: This voluminous silhouette embodies Ballard's signature aesthetic: quiet, introspective and deeply personal.

Opposite: Amid Berlin's avant-garde fashion scene, Olivia Ballard stands out by doing the opposite – embracing minimalism with a raw, emotional depth that feels almost radical in its restraint.

Her collection At Dusk, of January 2023, was a study in subtle transitions. With slip dresses that teetered between casual and formal, and evening wear that felt effortlessly wearable, it was Ballard's love letter to twilight – those in-between moments when day gives way to night.

By Autumn/Winter 2024, Ballard went deeper into intimacy with Le Lit (The Bed). This collection transformed everyday softness into high fashion: duvet-like jackets, mattress-inspired padding and drapes that mimicked the disarray of unmade sheets. It wasn't just a collection; it was a narrative of vulnerability and self-reflection.

Ballard's work strips fashion down to its essentials, celebrating craftsmanship and form. Each design feels like a meditation on what clothing can be: not just something to wear, but something to feel. She creates timeless pieces that resonate on a deeply human level, elevating simplicity into an art form. From asymmetrical denim vests to ruched jersey hoodies, every piece feels deliberate and personal.

Ballard's studio is more than a retail space, it's real proof of her approach to fashion, a sanctuary for creativity. The studio also doubles as a collaborative space, where clients can co-create custom pieces with Ballard herself. It's intimate, intentional and entirely aligned with her design philosophy: quiet power, executed perfectly.

Esther Perbandt – the avant-gardist of Berlin

Esther Perbandt stands out as one of the most distinctive voices in Berlin's fashion scene. Her commitment to designing exclusively in black and her refusal to follow conventional trends have made her a prominent figure in avant-garde fashion. Every piece she creates reflects a deep understanding of form and texture, using black as a canvas to explore emotion and structure in ways that transcend seasonal trends.

Perbandt's approach to fashion is deliberate and unapologetic. While others might compromise their aesthetic for broader appeal, she has always stayed true to her vision. Critics have often questioned her dedication to black, suggesting it could limit her reach. For Esther, black is not a restriction but a challenge, and one that fuels her creativity. Through layers, cuts and intricate details, she turns monochrome into a language that speaks to strength and individuality.

Esther Perbandt's designs fuse Berlin's raw edge with poetic tailoring, crafting a monochrome world where androgyny and rebellion reign.

Esther gained international recognition when she appeared on a US television design competition, a stage where designers often feel pressure to conform to mainstream expectations. Throughout the competition, she was repeatedly encouraged to soften her aesthetic or introduce colour. Instead, she stood firm, showcasing the power of her minimalist yet bold approach. Her eventual victory was a testament to the resonance of her work and the value of staying authentic, even in spaces dominated by commercialized standards. Her collections strike a balance between sharp tailoring and more fluid, deconstructed elements. The designs evoke Berlin's dualities – modern and historic, structured and chaotic, refined yet raw. They reflect the spirit of a city that thrives on contrasts and challenges norms.

Esther's influence extends beyond her collections. She has become a symbol of Berlin's ethos in fashion: daring, independent and deeply rooted in personal expression. Her work continues to inspire others to see fashion as a space for authenticity and creative exploration rather than mere adherence to fleeting trends.

Opposite: Esther Perbandt's A/W 2017 show at Volksbühne theatre during fashion week.

Overleaf: A sculptural black gown with razor-sharp tailoring – Esther Perbandt turns Berlin's underground grit into pure, cinematic drama.

chapter 7

SECOND-HAND

THE SECOND-HAND AND CONCEPT SCENE

Second-hand shopping is a philosophy in Berlin. It's not about trends, it's about individuality, history and defiance against the culture of fast fashion. For Berliners, finding one of a kind via vintage is a ritual, an art form and, sometimes, a competitive sport. In a city where identity is everything, second-hand shopping gives people the tools to craft their unique story, so you see how much this matters.

A culture of uniqueness

Berliners don't want to blend in. They want their clothes to speak, to challenge, to subvert. Wearing a vintage coat from the 70s or reworking a military jacket found in a flea market isn't just about aesthetics, it's a form of self-expression. The city's love for second-hand fashion is rooted in its history. After the war, when resources were scarce, people in Berlin made do with what they had. Clothes were repurposed, patched and given new life. This was obviously a necessity, but it was also resilience. That same scrappy, resourceful energy lives on today. Walking into a vintage shop in Berlin isn't like walking into a regular store. It feels more like a treasure hunt. Each rack is filled with possibilities – silhouettes that whisper stories, textures that demand a closer look and labels that transport you to another era. The thrill lies in the unknown, in uncovering that one item that feels like it was waiting just for you.

Berlin's second-hand market is thriving.

In recent years, the global fashion industry's shift towards sustainability has made second-hand shopping even more significant. Berliners aren't buying vintage just for style – they're making a statement. With the climate crisis looming, second-hand shopping offers a tangible way to opt out of the wastefulness of fashion. It's about slowing down, consuming less and cherishing what you already have. Berliners pride themselves on their ability to spot quality, even in a pile of cast-offs. A well-made leather jacket, a perfectly distressed pair of Levi's, a dress with intricate hand-stitched details – these aren't just clothes. They're investments, pieces meant to last for decades, not months.

The second-hand scene

Berlin is a city of contrasts, and its vintage stores reflect this beautifully. From high-end curated spaces to chaotic treasure troves, there's a second-hand experience for everyone. Here are some of the must-visit spots in Berlin for anyone serious about vintage.

- **Homefullofclothes:** This vintage and second-hand store is a love letter to Berlin's quirky, unpolished charm. The racks are filled with carefully selected pieces that feel both nostalgic and futuristic. Expect to find oversized knits, perfectly worn-in denim, and accessories that feel straight out of a '90s film. This store celebrates the imperfect and the unexpected, qualities that feel quintessentially Berlin.

The city's second-hand scene is setting the rules for street style.

Homefullofclothes' carefully curated selection.

- **Final Layer:** For those who love minimalism with an edge, Final Layer is a must. The aesthetic here is more refined, with a focus on clean lines, muted tones and impeccable craftsmanship. Think vintage Margiela, Prada and Helmut Lang mixed with no-name labels that look just as striking. It's the kind of place where you leave with a piece you'll wear for years. Extremely curated, extremely aesthetic, carefully curated archival pieces that attract fashion collectors from all over the world.

- **Sing Blackbird Vintage:** More than a vintage store, this Kreuzberg gem is a hub for creativity and connection. The selection leans toward feminine silhouettes with a touch of whimsy – floral dresses, velvet jackets and accessories that feel like they belong in a fairytale. It's a place where shopping feels joyful, not transactional. One of Berlin's OG gems.

- **Wsiura:** Hidden in the heart of Neukölln, Wsiura feels like a secret you want to keep to yourself. The aesthetic is unapologetically bold, with a mix of '80s power suits, avant-garde pieces and grunge-inspired finds. It's the kind of place where you walk in looking for a sweater and leave with a floor-length leather gown – and no regrets.

An ensemble put together from Sing Blackbird's collection of vintage.

The thrill of the hunt

Part of the magic of second-hand shopping is the hunt. It's about sifting through racks of clothes, searching for that one item that makes your heart race. It's about patience, intuition and a little bit of luck. The process is as rewarding as the find itself. Every vintage piece comes with a story, a past and a sense of mystery. *Who wore this before you? Where has it been? What memories are stitched into its seams?* In Berlin, this thrill is amplified by the city's abundance of flea markets (Flohmärkte), vintage fairs and hidden gems. Places like Flohmarkt am Mauerpark or the RAW Flohmarkt are legendary for their eclectic mix of fashion, art and oddities. They're places where you can lose yourself for hours, discovering pieces you didn't even know you needed.

Berlin's flea markets on a Sunday morning.

For those deeply embedded in Berlin's second-hand scene, shopping isn't just about clothes – it's about community. As Berlin's fashion scene continues to evolve, its commitment to second-hand shopping and community-driven concept stores remains steadfast. These spaces represent the city's values: sustainability, individuality and a refusal to conform. They're a reminder that fashion doesn't have to be wasteful or exclusive. It actually can be thoughtful, inclusive and deeply personal. Second-hand shopping is Berlin's love language, its way of saying, "You matter. Your story matters. Wear it proudly."

Concept stores – community meets curation

While vintage stores are the backbone of Berlin's second-hand scene, concept stores add another layer to the city's fashion ecosystem. These spaces aren't just about selling clothes – they're about creating a lifestyle, a community and a dialogue around fashion.

- **VOO Store Berlin**: This Kreuzberg institution is more than a store, it's a meeting place for Berlin's fashion-forward crowd. With a curated selection of designer pieces, streetwear and home goods, VOO blends high fashion with the city's casual edge. The café inside offers a space to linger, connect and people-watch. What sets VOO apart is its commitment to showcasing local talent alongside global brands. It's a reminder that Berlin's fashion scene is as much about fostering creativity as it is about celebrating it.

- **Highsnobiety Store:** Known globally as a media powerhouse, Highsnobiety's Berlin flagship brings its editorial vision to life. More than a store, it's a reflection of the brand's ethos – where streetwear, high fashion, interior and culture collide. The space feels like a gallery, with each piece carefully displayed to tell a story. It's a place where fashion enthusiasts and culture buffs come together, united by a shared love for innovation and individuality.

- **Andreas Murkudis:** Andreas Murkudis is the kind of space that makes you want to quit fast fashion forever – or at least consider doing so. Tucked away in a clean, industrial space that somehow feels warmer than your favourite sweater, the store is a temple to curation. Every item feels like it's been hand-picked with a borderline obsessive eye for detail. This isn't just another concept store – this is the dream shopping experience for anyone who wants to be surrounded by objects that feel important. You'll find everything from crisp, understated pieces by Lemaire to impossibly chic ceramics that scream functional art. The vibe? Quiet luxury without pretension. You walk in and suddenly feel like you need to re-evaluate your whole wardrobe, your home, maybe even your life. Murkudis doesn't just sell clothes or objects; he sells a lifestyle – one where every detail is deliberate, every choice intentional. And for Berliners who pride themselves on looking like they don't care (even when they do), this place is pure gold.

Above: The city's best curated vintage and concept resale stores treat fashion like an archive, displaying pre-owned pieces with the same reverence as a museum.

Overleaf: Berlin's vintage scene has gained international attention for its ability to blur the line between thrift and high fashion. It's not about nostalgia: it's about rewriting the rules of luxury.

- **Darklands:** Walking into Darklands feels less like shopping and more like stepping into a dystopian art installation, and that's exactly the point. This is more than a store; it's a mood, a world unto itself. Known for its stark aesthetic and uncompromising vision, Darklands curates some of the most avant-garde pieces in the game. Think Rick Owens, Boris Bidjan Saberi and Julius, all masters of the dark, the sculptural, the other-worldly. This isn't the place to look for wardrobe staples; it's where you find that one jaw-dropping piece that makes you feel invincible. The space itself is as much a part of the experience as the clothes, with its raw, industrial vibe and a deliberate air of mystery. Darklands doesn't just sell clothes; it sells a perspective, a way of seeing yourself in the world. For those who live and breathe the Berlin underground aesthetic, this store is a shrine. It's iconic, and the kind of place that makes you question everything you thought you knew about fashion and which forces you to take a moment to appreciate craftsmanship.

- **Endyma:** Endyma is a living, breathing archive dedicated to the genius of Helmut Lang. Nestled away from the chaos, it's where fashion nerds and minimalism devotees make their pilgrimage. This isn't about trend-chasing or flexing the latest logo – it's about understanding the DNA of modern fashion. Lang's work set the blueprint for the sleek, understated cool that so many designers try (and fail) to replicate today. What makes Endyma stand out is the obsessive curation. Each piece feels sacred, from the iconic bondage straps to the perfectly tailored suiting that redefined '90s minimalism. It's more than just a collection; it's a testament to Lang's vision, a vision that feels just as radical now as it did decades ago. The space itself mirrors the brand's ethos: sharp, clean and refined. For anyone serious about fashion's legacy and its ongoing influence, Endyma is the place where you can learn about it. And also, you can shop some of it.

LACOSTE
Gucci

chapter 8

BERLIN'S LEGACY

A MOVEMENT NOT A MOMENT

Berlin isn't trying to be Paris, Milan or London. This city doesn't aim to dazzle with unattainable glamour or feed into the elite, closed-door exclusivity that defines most fashion capitals. Berlin's fashion ethos isn't about perfection, it's about the raw, unfiltered reality of what it means to live in a city that has repeatedly reinvented itself from the rubble up. Berliners don't dress for approval. They dress to tell a story, and it's usually one of survival, rebellion and individuality. From the decadent cabaret looks of the 1930s to the gritty, anti-fashion statements of the 1990s, and the inclusive, community-driven concepts that dominate today's fashion scene, Berlin has proven itself to be less of a fashion capital and more of a cultural epicentre where clothes are just the starting point.

Let's talk about legacy – because Berlin doesn't play the trend game. It doesn't dress for the red carpet or the approval of front-row editors. Instead, it's a city that is built a fashion narrative that thrives on subversion, rejects the status quo and pulls its strength from the people, not the institutions. The city's love affair with second-hand shopping speaks volumes. In Berlin, it's not about having the latest It bag; it's about finding a 40-year-old leather jacket that tells its own history. This isn't nostalgia for the sake of it – it's a deliberate rejection of fast fashion and a celebration of individuality. Places like Homefullofclothes and Wsiura don't just sell clothes; I dare to say they curate identities. Berliners wear their independence as visibly as their clothes, creating a scene that feels deeply personal and profoundly political.

A clear example of a city where style is an act of defiance; the only rule is that there are none.

This is a city that's turned leather harnesses, oversized hoodies and military boots into a global language of rebellion, which has inspired people from all over the world. Designers like Rick Owens and Raf Simons understood this, borrowing from Berlin's gritty aesthetic to inject their collections with a rawness that screams authenticity. Yet Berlin doesn't seem to care about being an influencer, and maybe that's its secret. The best ideas here are born in basements, flea markets and dark clubs – not corporate boardrooms.

Kilian Kerner S/S 25 during Berlin Fashion Week.

Then there's the high-concept side of Berlin, places like Andreas Murkudis and Endyma that take curation to the level of artistry. These aren't stores – they're experiences. They embody a quieter rebellion, one that values craftsmanship and intentionality over flashiness. Murkudis invites you to rethink consumption altogether, while Endyma digs deep into the archives of Helmut Lang, showing us that true innovation often looks deceptively simple. Berlin is a city of contrasts, and these spaces embrace that tension: luxury meets utility, minimalism collides with excess, and history shapes the present without controlling it.

Berlin's fashion industry, if you can even call it that, thrives because it refuses to operate like a traditional industry. Berlin Fashion Week, for example, isn't about joining the ranks of the Big Four. It's about breaking the mould entirely. Runways in abandoned warehouses and shows that blur the lines between fashion, art and activism are more Berlin's speed. This isn't a city that puts gloss over cracks; it amplifies them. The result? Fashion that doesn't just look good but which means something. Berlin's take on sustainability, too, isn't a marketing gimmick, it's a way of life born out of decades of resourcefulness. It's about doing more with less and making it look effortlessly cool while you're at it.

What sets Berlin apart from other cities is its sense of community. Fashion here isn't about gatekeeping; it's about connecting. Stores like VOO and Sing Blackbird Vintage aren't just places to shop – they're gathering points for like-minded people who want to talk about design, art and culture. Berlin's inclusivity isn't performative; it's woven into the city's fabric. Whether it's DIY couture born in the thrift stores or experimental designs from young brands like Namilia, the city feels like it's constantly rewriting the rules to include more people, more perspectives, more voices.

But let's not romanticize Berlin too much. This is a city that thrives on contradictions. For all its grit and rebellion, it's also been complicit in its own cycles of commercialization. The tension between staying true to its underground roots and catering to a global audience is palpable. Berlin wants to be authentic, but authenticity has a habit of becoming marketable. Even its second-hand and concept stores sometimes flirt with exclusivity, pushing up prices and turning community-focused spaces into tourist hotspots. Berlin's challenge will always be navigating that line – staying raw without becoming a caricature of itself. But that's not just Berlin. Fashion, in all of its shapes, tries constantly to balance the purity of creative expression with the need to commercialize and grow, to sustain itself without losing the soul of what makes that art matter in the first place.

Ultimately, Berlin's fashion scene is a reflection of the city itself: messy, defiant and constantly evolving. It doesn't cater to the polished perfectionism of traditional fashion capitals, and that's why it resonates so deeply with a generation that values individuality over conformity. Berlin's story isn't just about clothes – it's about the people who wear them, the spaces where they come alive, and the subcultures that keep pushing the city forward. Fashion here is never just about looking good; it's about feeling something. And isn't that the whole point?

Opposite: Berlin street style is effortless rebellion, where sharp tailoring clashes with underground edge, and fashion is less about fitting in and more about owning who you are.

Overleaf: Horror Vacui's S/S 25 show during Berlin Fashion Week turned the city into a romantic dreamscape: where nostalgia met modernity in a sea of delicate ruffles, intricate florals and heirloom-worthy silhouettes.

STONES

LOVE

INDEX

(Page numbers in *italic* refer to photographs)

CREDITS

The publishers would like to thank the following sources for their kind permission to reproduce the pictures in this book.

Alamy Stock Photo: Agencja Fotograficzna Caro 40-41, 52, 55; / dpa picture alliance 89, 96-97, 127, 130-131, 143; /Everett Collection Inc 28; /PA Images 70; /Studio Mostra 78; / Sueddeutsche Zeitung Photo 16-17, 58, 60-61, 74; /United Archives GmbH 76-77

Courtesy of Darklands, Berlin: 8, 144

Getty Images: John Aquino/Penske Media via Getty Images 68, 69; / Dominique Berretty/Gamma-Rapho via Getty Images 39; /Victor Boyko 86, 87; /Danigel/ullstein bild via Getty Images 32; /Volker Döring/ullstein bild via Getty Images 36; /Henrik Gaard/ ullstein bild via Getty Images 46; / Erich Engel/ullstein bild via Getty Images 27; /Giovanni Giannoni/ Penske Media via Getty Images 71, 84-85; /Martyn Goodacre/Getty Images 64-65; /Frazer Harrison 81, 112-113; / Hulton-Deutsch Collection/CORBIS/ Corbis via Getty Images 20; /Foc Kan/ WireImage 67; /Stefan Knauer/Getty Images for NEWEST at Namilia 115; / Keystone Features/Hulton Archive 23; /Alexander Koerner/Getty Images for IMG 128; /Ben Kriemann 146-147; /Franziska Krug/Getty Images for Marina Hoermanseder 102; /Jeremy Moeller 106; / Matthias Nareyek 103, 156-157; /Photo12/Universal Images Group via Getty Images 34-35; /Patrick Piel/Gamma-Rapho via Getty Images 43; /Regine Relang/ullstein bild via Getty Images 24; /Andreas Rentz 90-91; /Sebastian Reuter 110, 116-117, 120, 121, 122, 124, 125; /Sebastian Reuter/Getty Images for COLLECTIVEFOUR Danny Reinke 100-101, 152; /Sebastian Reuter/ Getty Images for Nowadays 94; /Jack Robinson/Hulton Archive 49; /Joshua Sammer/Getty Images for NEWEST Contemporay Fashion Hub 123; / Christian Simonpietri/Sygma via Getty Images 50-51; /Snapshot-photography/ ullstein bild via Getty Images 140; / Tollkühn/ullstein bild via Getty Images 63; /Tristar Media 118; /ullstein bild/ ullstein bild via Getty Images 7; Victor Virgile/Gamma-Rapho via Getty Images 80; /Christian Vierig 11, 99, 105, 108, 109, 155; /Wolfgang Wiese/ullstein bild via Getty Images 151; /Yva/ullstein bild via Getty Images 19

Courtesy of homefullofclothes: 135, 136, 138

Private Collection: 14

Shutterstock: Schneider-Press/Siebert/ SIPA: 82

Courtesy of Sing Blackbird: 139